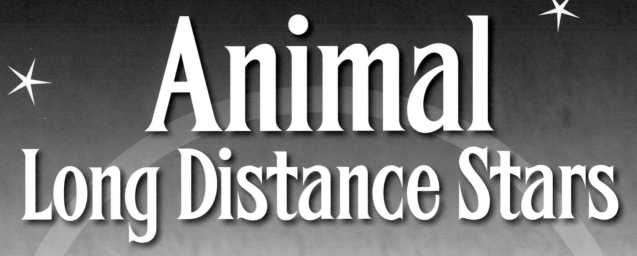

Animal
Long Distance Stars

BY SALLY MCGRAW

The Child's World®
childsworld.com

Published by The Child's World®
1980 Lookout Drive • Mankato, MN 56003-1705
800-599-READ • www.childsworld.com

Photographs ©: Grobler du Preez/iStockphoto, cover, 1; Incredible
Arctic/Shutterstock Images, 5; Fat Camera/iStockphoto, 6;
Aaron M. Sprecher/Gold Toe/AP Images, 7; Oleg Znamenskiy/
Shutterstock Images, 9, 21; iStockphoto, 10, 13, 20; Tony Smith
CC2.0, 14; Shutterstock Images, 17, 20–21; Paul S. Wolf/
Shutterstock Images, 18

ISBN 9781503820418
LCCN 2016960511

Printed in the United States of America
PA02341

ABOUT THE AUTHOR

Sally McGraw is a freelance writer, editor, and ghostwriter. She holds a creative writing degree from Binghamton University and has written books for children, teens, and adults on everything from ecology to fashion. She lives in Minneapolis with her husband and two goofy cats.

Contents

CHAPTER 1

Long Distance ★ Stars

How far can a human run without stopping? It depends on the runner's skill. It also depends on how fast that runner is going. For short distances, some humans can run as fast as 28 miles per hour (45 km/h). But for long distances, running slower works better. The runner can keep going without getting too tired.

The animal kingdom has many amazing long distance athletes. Some have long legs or wings to help them go far. All of them cool down their bodies quickly, so they don't overheat.

Why do these animals **migrate** so far? Some animals travel to give birth. Others migrate to escape cold weather.

Animals can run, swim, or fly to cover amazing distances.

A full marathon is 26.2 miles (42.16 km). On average, it takes 4 to 5 hours to complete. Ultrarunners run farther than that!

Some animals leave to find new food sources. Many animals return to the same place every year.

Humans do not migrate, but they can still run long distances. How would a talented human athlete compare to animal superstars?

Human **ultrarunners** run more than 26 miles (42 km) at a time. But Pam Reed once ran 300 miles (483 km) without stopping! It took her 80 hours. Pam also ran a 135-mile (217-km) ultramarathon. It was through Death Valley, in California. There, temperatures can soar to 120 degrees Fahrenheit (49 degrees Celsius). She's an amazing athlete! But how would she compare to long distance animal champions?

Three things will decide which animal is the best long distance athlete. How far does it travel? What kind of weather does it travel through? And what kind of **terrain** does it come cross? So, which animal would win the gold medal in the animal Olympics for long distance?

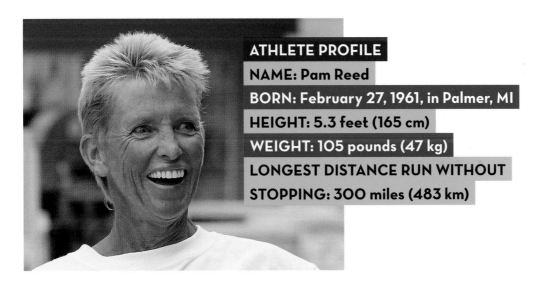

ATHLETE PROFILE
NAME: Pam Reed
BORN: February 27, 1961, in Palmer, MI
HEIGHT: 5.3 feet (165 cm)
WEIGHT: 105 pounds (47 kg)
LONGEST DISTANCE RUN WITHOUT STOPPING: 300 miles (483 km)

CHAPTER 2

★ Africa's Long-Legged Runners

Every year, 1.7 million blue wildebeests migrate across the Serengeti Plain in Tanzania. This is a country in eastern Africa. The wildebeests move up and down the plain all year long searching for fresh grass to eat. Wildebeests run together in giant herds. They have long legs and sturdy hooves that make them excellent long distance travelers. It may become very hot or rainy as they travel, but weather almost never stops their migration.

ANIMAL PROFILE
NAME: Blue Wildebeest
HEIGHT: 50 to 58 inches at the shoulder (127 to 147 cm)
WEIGHT: Up to 600 pounds (272 kg)
DISTANCE TRAVELED: 1,000 miles (1,609 km) per year

Blue wildebeests are also called gnus.

Blue wildebeests swim across rivers as quickly as possible.

Blue wildebeests usually walk or gallop slowly. But they can run up to 40 miles per hour (64 km/h) when they feel afraid. Many predators hunt them, including lions, cheetahs, and hyenas. Traveling in huge groups protects them, but it is also a weakness. If a predator scares the herd, many wildebeests will panic. Babies can get separated from their mothers. Adults can get hurt or killed, too.

Wildebeests climb cliffs as they migrate. They also swim across rivers. The wildebeests must cross rivers to find food. But some are eaten by crocodiles as they try to swim across. It is a dangerous journey for these amazing athletes.

Fun Fact

Blue wildebeest herds can be 25 miles (40 km) long as they cross the plains.

CHAPTER 3

Chasing Summer on White Wings

This small bird is a true long-distance superstar! Arctic terns migrate almost all year. They fly from Greenland to Antarctica and back again. They do not fly in a straight line. Their path makes a zigzag shape. They do this on purpose to avoid flying against strong winds.

Arctic terns hatch their eggs in in the northern hemisphere. Then they travel south for food. The tern can fly at speeds of 22 to 25 miles per hour (35 to 40 km/h).

ANIMAL PROFILE
NAME: Arctic Tern
LENGTH: 11 to 15 inches (28 to 38 cm)
WINGSPAN: 25 to 30 inches (64 to 76 cm)
WEIGHT: 3 to 4 ounces (85 to 113 g)
DISTANCE TRAVELED: Up to 40,000 miles (64,000 km) per year

Arctic terns will often travel out of the way just to avoid bad weather.

Arctic terns snatch fish out of the water. They also often scare other birds into dropping their prey so the arctic tern can eat it instead!

Because their journey takes so long and goes from the North Pole to the South Pole, they live through summer two times each year! This is because the seasons are reversed in the Northern and Southern Hemispheres. When it is winter in the United States, it is summer in countries south of the equator. The tern also migrates to follow warm summer weather.

Arctic terns eat mostly small fish, and their journey takes them along coastlines and across ocean waters. They are excellent fliers, but strong winds and storms can force them to stop flying. This is one of this champion's few weaknesses.

Fun Fact

Arctic terns can live to be more than 30 years old. During that time, a tern will migrate approximately 1.5 million miles (2.4 million km). That is equal to three trips to the moon and back!

CHAPTER 4

Underwater Travelers

Here's an animal athlete that swims long distances! Humpback whales make the longest journey of any **mammal** on Earth. They swim on average 1 mile per hour (1.5 km/h). They are very slow. But they travel thousands of miles every year to find food and have their babies.

Humpback whales are found in all oceans. During the summer, approximately 40,000 humpback whales migrate north. They come up from the Southern Hemisphere. Many travel near Alaska.

ANIMAL PROFILE
NAME: Humpback Whale
LENGTH: Up to 60 feet (18 m)
WEIGHT: 50,000 to 80,000 pounds (22,000 to 36,000 kg)
DISTANCE TRAVELED: An average of 6,000 miles (9,656 km) per year

Baby humpback whales are called calves.

Humpback whales often breach, or jump, out of the water. Scientists still aren't sure why!

In the north, they eat as much as they can to prepare for the journey south. Whales eat krill and plankton, which live mostly in cold water. Then they start swimming toward Hawaii or Mexico in the fall. They spend winter in the warm water. The whales do not eat much during the winter. They live off the fat they built up in summer. This can make them weak and slow as they begin to swim north again the following summer.

Mothers have their babies in winter. Then mothers and babies travel north together in summer. Migration is a family activity for humpback whales!

Humpback whales are also known for their unique call sounds. The whales' noises sound like songs. They have been known to sing for hours. Scientists aren't sure why the whales sing.

Fun Fact

The longest recorded humpback whale migration was 11,706 miles (18,839 km), from American Samoa to Antarctica.

CHAPTER 5

The Award Ceremony

GOLD MEDAL
Arctic Tern

SILVER MEDAL
Humpback Whale

Which of these animal long-distance athletes is the winner? The gold medal winner is the arctic tern! This bird travels seven times farther than the whale and 40 times farther than the wildebeest. The silver medal goes to the humpback whale for covering 6,000 miles (9,656 km). The bronze medal goes to the blue wildebeest!

BRONZE MEDAL
Blue Wildebeest

Glossary

mammal (MAM-uhl) A mammal is an animal that feeds its babies with milk a mother makes. Even though it lives underwater, the humpback whale is a mammal.

migrate (MY-grate) Animals that migrate travel long distances every year to find food or have babies. Blue wildebeests migrate across the Serengeti Plain.

terrain (tuh-RANE) Terrain is different kinds of land. Mountains, plains, forests, and deserts are all types of terrain.

ultrarunners (UHL-trah-ruhn-nurs) Ultrarunners are people who run very long distances in competitive races. Ultrarunners run more than 26 miles (42 km) without stopping.

To Learn More

In the Library

Carney, Elizabeth. *Great Migrations: Whales, Wildebeests, Butterflies, Elephants, and Other Amazing Animals on the Move.* Washington, DC: National Geographic, 2010.

Catt, Thessaly. *Migrating with the Arctic Tern.* New York, NY: PowerKids Press, 2011.

Cohn, Scotti. *On the Move: Mass Migrations.* Mount Pleasant, SC: Arbordale Publishing, 2013.

On the Web

Visit our Web site for links about animals that travel long distances: **childsworld.com/links**

Note to Parents, Teachers, and Librarians: We routinely verify our Web links to make sure they are safe and active sites. So encourage your readers to check them out!

Index